Shahad Almutahhar lives in Saudi Arabia and is currently a doctor in training. Her passion for writing started in primary school and she has always dreamed of becoming a published author. She has published a research article in the International Journal of Life Sciences and Pharma Research, and has more research articles on the way. Along with writing educational materials, Shahad enjoys writing poetry as a means of expression and sharing it with both readers and writers.

To Finn,
Without whom,
This would have never been.

Shahad Almutahhar

PHOENIX ABLAZE

AUSTIN MACAULEY PUBLISHERS™

LONDON * CAMBRIDGE * NEW YORK * SHARJAH

A CIP catalogue record for this title is available from the British Library.

ISBN 9781398499744 (Paperback)
ISBN 9781035803200 (ePub e-book)

www.austinmacauley.com

First Published 2023
Austin Macauley Publishers Ltd®
1 Canada Square
Canary Wharf
London
E14 5AA

I would firstly like to thank Austin Macauley Publishers for making this book

come true, and their help in making sure it reaches the hands of my readers.

I would also like to extend my appreciation to my family and friends who helped

me in making this book a reality.

Last but certainly not least, I would like to thank YOU. Yes, the person who is

holding or listening to this book. Wherever you are and whoever you are, I am

so glad my book has reached you, and I hope it was a memorable read.

Table of Contents

Puppeteer

Sunny day
And rainy clouds
Humming birds
And buzzy stingers

The golden sand warms my toes
The lively waves lead me to a star that glows
For I am sleet's canvas
Now fully encompassed

A black mob
Which strings have laced between my limbs
Have danced through my hair
And kissed my eyes

Veins of struggle present at my neck
Tears of fear wet my cheeks
A coppery substance fills my taste buds
Promising treasures that trick the greatest of minds

Sapped of my strength
Knocked of my will
And now stolen of every skill
I am back, yes indeed, I am back

Back to square one
Where the skies are always furious
And the grounds are injurious
I am the black mob's puppet.

Red Dot

A look at your right
A look at your left
One petal there
Another here

Robbed of your sight
Granting you forever night
Not a glimpse of the doer
Another victim of a voyeur

Love bites at your skin
Little do you know of the sin
The coldness of the night
Draws you to the light

One petal
Two petals, three
Oh, the beauty we are oblivious to

A beating heart
A dying rose
An innocence goes
With the singular red dot, in a sea of darkness.

Intangible Butterflies

A screen in front of my eyes
Visualising the thoughts after my temples
Behind bars, I watch as all go by

Intangible butterflies
They fly concealed
Soaring to unhidden realms

I watch as all go by
Not a word can be spoken
For the spell mustn't be broken

Try as I might
But the words aren't obtainable
For they have been stolen

Intangible butterflies
They fly concealed within the darkness
With my words, forever stealing my ability to express.

Phoenix on Fire

In the golden feather went
Illuminating chambers that have never slept
Beleaguering the old and the liverish

The pain that was ethereal
Leaving her ephemeral
Was wandering through the perishing shells

The fire roared and soared through crimson blood
Inside blue eyes
Hindering anyone's ability to recognise

What once was a frozen angel at the exterior
And a kindling fire at the heart
Was swallowed up whole

Dead and dying
Her inner fire eating her away
Sending redolent mists to the sky

All of it her own making
Leaving her kin in a daze
The phoenix was left ablaze.

Her mellifluous songs never again heard amongst the jays.

Yearn*

You've left me in the folds of dubiety
Erasing my ability to recognise abuse
And leaving me trapped behind indecisive bars
Relinquishing your soft fingers and beautiful mind
Night and day, you've left me in a yearning trance.

Sin

My dear mister
Eyes afire
And a frozen heart
As powerful as life.

My darling,
Drain my bleeding ribs,
Eat my hollow heart
Just save me a platter of life
'cause all you're making me do is sin
With your face between my thighs
And my thumb on your lips.

Mister, mister
Take me with you
Up high inside the scorching sun
And in between the realms of your home

My long friend,
Take my hand
In a velvet box
And unleash my soul to the unknown.

Devil, my faithful lover
Give me your eyes
And take my being
Because your love's so warm

I can taste the ashes of my skin
And feel the burning of my heart.

Where have you hidden my childhood?
You've imprisoned my memories
And sliced the frown out of my mask

'cause all you're making me do is sin
With my hand on your chest
And your thumb between my lips.

Lovely mister,
Do look at me
And give me a piece of you

A piece of your bloody life
A taste of your wicked mind
And a feeling of your love

Hold my hand, take me with you
Away from the sun
Into the dark,
Between the realms of your home
Keep me safely hidden.

Baby, all you're making me do is sin
But I'm in a trance, forever locked.

Dear mister devil, My friend
My lover
Please hide me here
Inside the folds of your hatred
Away from the final sleep
Because I'm forever yours to keep.

The Blues

The blues are nothing but the seasonal cold to the mind,
A depressive wave growing as it approaches
I could make it out in the distance
Oh, how the hot sun blazed its outlines
And the ice gave it crystal powers
It grew mightier as it approached
Yet it caught me by surprise
As it hit me with its cries
Telling me this is nothing
But a ripple in the ocean.

Depression

Pearls and jewels
Golds and silvers
White, red, blue, and green
Glamorise my body

I hate how ungrateful I am
Dreaded feelings of despair
Dancing through the air
A luxurious ocean flowing through my feet

Thought that I could chase these feelings away
The petals of my heart
Have polluted the grounds
They have stained my ribs

My blood is dripping
Into the ocean it disappears
Escaping through my fingers
It's falling out of my grasp

My tears
They flow and fly
They run and race
My tears, they can't find their way out

Is that you?
I can hear your footsteps
I can smell your stench
Oh, how dreaded the sight of you is

Is that really you?
Tiptoeing through the corridors of my memories
Using your fingers of silk,
I believe the magic tricks enforced on me.

Knots

Keenly, I await your magician fingers
Nobody visualises your talent
Orally, you've left me in a trance
Tie my ends together
Sever my wounds

You've formed a knot
Inside my heart
You've tied my arteries and veins
You've stopped my blood

You've formed a knot
In my brain
You've tied my neurons from end to end
You've paralysed me

At the back of your studio
I am left forgotten
So full of knots
A mystery awaiting magician minds.

I Love You*

I am in deep need of your companionship.

Little do you know
Of the nights I spend impatient
Vividly I dream
Every night I have one fear

Your face fading into the void
Over the darkness I no longer recognise you
Under the bed I cry and mourn, over a friend who may no longer be.

The Killer in Me

I collapse
When I dive this deep
Fold inwards this much

When you can see my insides
I get so sick of myself
You can't hold me accountable

I like using a geometric compass
To draw arcs and circles
To create a map on your back

I like to see you smile
Your fugacious watery eyes
I love to hear you howl

Let me tattoo your body
With knives and jewels
Let me expose your glamour, see your efflorescence

A tear by your ear
A hawk nesting on your collarbone
A crime you don't know of

Give me the power,
let me make you a cynosure
I love who I hurt
Let me give you a treat,

Open your eyes
Watch for my lagniappe to you

Let me give you a treat
Open your eyes
Let me scar your mind and feed my ebullience

How could I hurt who I love
I will mutilate you, your dulcet face
Wake up every morning and you are my chandelier
Because I do love you.

And I will never stop
Because this isn't a dalliance
This is sempiternal.

Drowning in a pool of darkness
At your feet you watch me fade
Into the depths you let me go

A fingertip at your ankle goes unnoticed
For your eyes look to the sky
To the victories awaiting

A cry for help goes unnoticed
For your mind is set to thrive
To succeed is its only drive

Swallowed whole, I swim with the angels
In my heart, I am betrayed
Forever in your life displayed.

From the heavens above I look at you
Your vague dreams I turn to nightmares
Going about with unshed tears

Locking you in oblivion, your sanity forever stolen
Forgotten by your wife
And trapped with me in the afterlife

After all, aren't I your most prized success?

Stupid Joke

Of the stupid joke
I sit and wonder
Of the time unspent
I cry and mourn

In a glimpse he was here
By my side
He'd make me laugh
In his back, a scar he'd try to hide

Come morning
He was missing
Sat in my bed, I am reminiscing
Where exactly was he hurting?

Not a word
To friend or foe
Up in heaven or down in hell, for all I know
His true self, forever a mystery

I sit and wonder
Of the stupid joke
Regretting never asking
Why his back he's always hiding.

Reckless, Reckless

Jumping mountain tops
Being chased by cops
Her many identities she swaps

Graffiti on bridges
Halloween pranks in the streets
Homework she never completes

Reckless, reckless
She is
Reckless, reckless

Bloodshot eyes
About her grades she lies
A smiley face you think is wise

A runny nose
Between clouds of euphoria she arose
With a broken heart she goes

Suicidal, suicidal
She is
Suicidal, suicidal.

Freedom

Rusty metal eating its way into her skin
A coppery taste powders her senses
After all these years, leaving her senseless

Drip, drip, drip
A puddle at her feet
Her reflection, she sees is beat

Outside where the birds harmonise
And the healthy exercise
A happy atmosphere you easily recognise

She smiles
Takes on her captivity for the last time
And never shows up for suppertime

She is locked behind bars
But now her mind is free
And it soars the valleys and hills of freedom.

The Reality of Life

Are these friends?
They're always pretending,
Depending and sometimes even bullying.

Is this a family?
Always pointing out your flaws,
And extending their claws.

Are these teachers?
Always laughing,
Torturing and even backbiting.

Is this life?
It seems more like a hunting knife.

One post a day
Keeps the insanity away.

Witness

Up all night, you had me waiting
Entranced by your mystery
I was frozen in place

You smiled
Never tried
But always lied

You took the little girl and gave her some pop
Carving a moon out of your flesh
You gave her a souvenir to cherish

You set her free
And let her stroll while you counted three
Then you struck her knee

All while I was the one to see
How you never set her free
And witness how you had her for supper near a tree.

Accept

Please accept this gift I leave
In your hands let it grieve

Hold it to the sun, see it flourish
I trust my gift, you will nourish

Wet it with your tears
Give it love, don't let it witness your scares

For it is my beating heart
In your hands, because it and I must be kept apart

Please accept this gift I leave
Accept this beating heart who's left to grieve.

Rich Garden

Tick tock, tick tock
In the waiting area you're in shock
Of the many different people in stock

The old lady who wishes everyone a good morning
Upon her arrival
But is readily snoring, with her sunglasses on, in a wheelchair

The man who's holding a newspaper
Which he isn't reading
But instead is slightly dozing off, after a long night with his lover

The little girl who won't stop talking
About the many friendships of which she is in the making
And the teddy she "only bought just yesterday"

And that boy, dressed in neon
Sitting in the corner, fidgeting all the time
He's definitely on porn

You go for a sip of water
Overwhelmed by the varieties of flowers
In the waiting area

Only one empty seat, you're dumbfounded
Nobody wants to sit next to an edgy teen on porn
But there you're forced to sit, by your aching joints

Curiosity getting the best of you
That poor boy is reading goodnight texts between him and his boyfriend
On the edge of tears, for his cancerous lover

You sit back in awe and wonder
Of the rich garden
Present in the hospital waiting area.

The Dreadful Word

The dreadful word
The act of bravery
Putting you at the risk of treachery

On a tight rope
With a raging ocean of fire underneath
Can you utter the dreadful word?

Open your mouth
Slightly exhale
To utter that dreadful word

A sign of weakness
You think strength is a sign of uniqueness
And your determination is slowly withering away

On your office floor, you're bleeding out
Anything, indeed you'd do anything
Not to utter the dreadful word and ask for help.

Captivity

She got tired of
Being held in captivity
Because of
Her disability,
But all she ever showed
Were smiles
And the sense of gratitude,
But no one knew
That she's only living
To gratify,
And in doing so she's trying
To keep in the limits of quietude,
Wishing
Day and night
That the rain
Would wash over
Her problems
To cease
Their existence.

Survive

Blue jays singing a harmony
Blue petals dancing to their melody
His blue eyes an ocean of secrets

Salty dew leaves a glazed surface
The tree cries honey for her lost grace
He skips to the beat of demon cries

The leaves rustled for a victory
The pebbles uncovered a path delightedly
He was sun-kissed approvingly

He is wise
Maybe full of lies
He is the mysterious survivor, whom I aspire to be.

Addict

I hate the perfect liar I have become
When the truth burns my lips
And fights to be freed
I hate the liar I have become
Seeking revenge,
The truth ignites and rages
Taking its life along with mine
The truth is a pyromaniac
A raging fire, taking all my insides with it
And I burn, burn, burn
And through it all I can't help but think
How much I hate the perfect liar I have become
Yet I still lie and always will
Because an addict is a prisoner
Gazing at freedom behind bars
But is a fool to think that what they have is far better than freedom
And I hate the perfect liar I have become
Because it's turned me into the addict I am today and will be till my last day.

Scorpion

Jewelled eyes
A sweet tongue
And an ivory touch

Come forth, I am called
In your grasp,
I am appalled I can see it all

You're deadly in the eyes
So full of lies
And my life you are taking, like the many different lives

In me, you've planted your stinger
Swimming through the depths of deception
In your arms,
I do not wish to linger.

Fat Cat

Hitler was a twat
Britney Spears is such a brat
I wear a stupid hat
I sit and wonder why you are as low as a bat
And you wonder why I'm so fat.
To the skies and beyond, I gaze at the star you once were
Our once sacred bond, I see the scar that you bear.
Appalled at what I have become, I hide my tears
Enthralled by what I have done, I give into my fears.

It Has Begun

In the autumn winds
I am beginning to whither
In the darkness of the night
I am starting to shiver

Amidst the angry trees
I see a face
In my mind,
I am lost in space
Frightened by a sound
I wish to be hidden underground

A poke on my side
A breeze on my shoulder
The trees coalesce into one
The ending has begun.

It's Funny

It's funny,
They tell you
You're their favourite,
Yet they're never in sight
When you're most needy.

It's funny,
They claim they worry,
Yet they never bothered to ask if you were really fine.

It's funny,
They say they love you,
Yet they always shove you
To the others and all around.
It's funny,
They've said that they're here to help,
Yet they always brush you off
Telling you they're busy.

It's funny,
They said you're full of apprehension,
Yet they never showed a bit of attention.
It's funny,
Because they don't really care
They were just being fake,
Tossing you around
And silently watching as you were clowned.

Remain

At six,
You were so sure you'd never die
And I was dead certain I'd never get high

At ten,
You'd never make it past auditions for the football team
And I failed in helping you fulfil a dream

At fourteen,
A drunk you kissed a sober me
And I could've sworn that kiss stained my memory till yesterday

At twenty-one,
You drank so much that you waltzed right into death's grasp
And ever since, I haven't been a day clean

Liar, liar
Whether Gods or Devils
We remain liars on all the levels

Unfit to compete,
Everyday a cheat
We are forced to comply.

How can I stand up when
There's no one to hold me when I fall?

How can I stand up when
I am being pushed to the ground by the closest people of all?

How can I stand up when
I am all alone
Away I've been thrown
Just like an abandoned toy?

Stop telling me to stay strong
To fight or to prolong,
Because you, alone, are the one
Destroying all of me.

Grey Life

You're not happy, that's for sure
What if you're sad, but isn't that just for the poor?
You think you're worried but then you notice that bit of anger tugging at the edge
of your soul.

Happy? No
Sad? No
Bored? Yes, but isn't that just a synonym for numb??

Fading into a grey world.
Grey clouds
And shrouds.
Grey oceans
And emotions,
Grey minds
And grey souls.

She dies of anorexia,
He suffers from pneumonia,
They cry of guilt
And laugh of glee.

But you,
You with the grey hair
And a life unfair,
You,
You with stick limbs
And a cotton brain,

You with a gummy tongue
And rock teeth,
You with crystal, rare tears
Without even peers.
Living a grey,
Grey life.

Society

With eyes piercing into
Her torn soul,
They judged her.

Overusing criticisms,
They forever damaged her
Crushing her high hopes and self-esteem.

Extending their sharpened claws,
They playfully
Scarred her once soft skin.

Using jagged words,
They jokingly
Sliced her into bits.

Offer

I'll get to know you,
Your gestures
Will uncover your hidden lies.

I'll get to know you,
Your deep emotions
Will dance across your eyes.

I'll get to know you,
By the way you talk,
How words slide across your tender lips.

I'll get to know you,
Because the rest of you
Won't participate in your play at hiding.

And when I know you,
I won't offer you a hiding spot
Because stars shine and do not hide.

Young

All the young souls sat on rooftops
Wishing to find beauty in their before
Or for beauty to find its way in their after.

Absorb

It's a horrible feeling
For someone to give you their all
And for you to have nothing to give in return

She said it hurts day and night
To spend it all loving you
When she knew you couldn't even give her a minute in return

With a mangled heart
He spent days on end
Sulking in avarice and pain

Wishing for a change
Wishing to be a new somebody
Wishing to carve his heart out and trade it for another

Yesterday he promised to absorb her pain
But today,
Today he's helpless because absorbing that pain would mean wiping himself
from her memory.

Mr Serial Killer

Mr serial killer was asked to fulfil the job of a babysitter
Poor little Tyler died on the hands of a baby killer
Behave, behave said he feeling so full of skill and experience

At 7 o'clock on Christmas Eve
While his parents were out sipping vodka
He was fighting in a pool of disbelief

He lost his hope
At the touch of a rope
With no sight of the thief
Who left him nothing but grief

At the funeral
To show up is what the killer chose
With a few tears
And a black rose.

Wilting Rose

Your hair,
A mess with no repair
Your mind,
An ocean of despair

Your eyes
Are crystal lies,
Your lips
Are sunken ships

Your nails leave bloody trails
Marking your arms with horror tales,
And your neck,
What a bruised wreck

Your stomach is a hollow pit
Waiting for your soul to submit
Yet you still hold on to the wilting rose
That is me.

The Present

School is the vampire searching the streets at nightfall,
Eyes a burning fire
Fangs dripping of desire

There came a time when,
My chest hurt
My heart missed a beat

Teachers are lying preachers
Roaming high above many creatures
In high need of a bleacher

There came a time when,
I was alert
But my life missed a week

Parents are busy under the mistletoe
They are nothing but the foe
With everything but love to show.

Deathbed

With tears in her eyes
She prayed,

With blood in his mouth
He fought,

With a bullet in her heart
She shot,

With a broken rib
He stood, head held high

With stolen purity
She isolated herself,

With a scarred brain
He wrote a letter,

With her last breath
She smiled.

Unseen Garden

Hair is fading
Numbers are falling
And gravity is failing

Music reaching the sky
Voices are up so high
To drown the supply

Skies are crying
The sun is lost
So the moon is dead

Rhythm of the beat
Our hearts are craving
Heroin injections are what we need

Roses are wilting
Flowers are guilty
And petals are endangered

Words cutting the clouds
Letters so sharp,
Bleeding overcrowds

Pink grass
Pale clouds,
Dead skies
This garden of mine houses many lives.

She

A heart
Of ventricles and atriums
Lungs
Of flesh and air
Blood
Of oxygen and antitoxin

But her, she was different.

With a heart
Of paper and metal
Lungs
Of smoke and coke
And blood
Of whiskey and ghosts

She was everything but human
'cause she weighed an ugly healthy
Ate tasty thoughts
And drank agonising screams

For Prince Charming liked curves
And society liked sticks.

The 5 Ws

Why is it that they are
Everything I am not,
Why is it that they get
Everything that I want
And why am I so far away from you?

When was the sky so blue
Why are your veins so blocked
Just how is it all so true?

Where is your cherry-red heart
Where are the bright blue eyes,
Where is my old you?

How are you so changed
How is this the same me
How did you drift so far?

When were your dreams askew
When did you get so harsh
What am I to do now?

Who is this new you,
Tell me,
Who stole the life from you?

The Other Dimension

The other dimension
Behind mirrors
And under rivers

With divorced eyes
Married hands
And separate feet

The other dimension
Inside walls
And within falls

With daily months
Hourly minutes
And yearly seconds

The other dimension
Of many dimensions
Lies within your tears.

With wailing skies
Black clouds
And crying wounds

The other dimension
Where people choke on air
And drink their bloody lives away

The other dimension
Of many dimensions
Lies within your tears.

The Light

I keep my tears in a velvet box
Carved in blood
And draped in silk
I keep my tears in the dark,

I keep my voice in a metal box
Carved in thoughts
And draped in shadows
I keep my voice in the dark,

I keep my hands in golden cuffs
Carved in hatred
And draped in love
I keep my hands in the dark,

I keep my brain in a silver sink
Carved in toxin
And draped in venom
I keep my brain in the dark,

I keep you in my heart
Carved in beauty
And draped in life
I keep you in the light.

I Require, I Desire

What I want
Is for stress to eat me up
And death to bury me alive
Right in front of your eyes

Black nails at my ribs
And bloody fangs
At my heart
With nothing but hunger in the eyes

I want oblivion
I'm the queen
In a sea of fish
Where you're the king

In your memories
I don't want to be
Because in your hands
Is where you hide me

You've carved my insides
And drowned my mind
But this is what I require
Because this is what I desire

Have my blood
Under your fingernails
And my eyeball
In your vodka

Tear me apart
Leave nothing in my heart
This is what I require
Because this is what I desire

Your tail wrapped around my neck
Screaming your prayer
I get your wrath
For your love is only in my sleep

Your blood between my lips
A heart between my hands
Your body forgotten
Under your favourite chair

This is what I require
Because this is what I desire
For you to no longer breathe
Your eyes forever closed.

Imprisoned

She only tried to show sympathy,
But her soul always stayed filthy
Bursting with all the sins,
The sins she's committed
It's like she's addicted,
Infecting everybody
Oh, the virus she's transmitted
Keeping me imprisoned
Locked by bars of hatred,
Bars of ignorance.

Candle

You're precious darling
You're so very precious
They all want a bite
God how precious is this site
And to you they must show all the care.

So come here
Step forward dear
Let me show you to the wonderland
Where everyone gets a bite
Where everyone will set you alight
Till your end you'll be the beautifully glowing candle.

Invisible but Deadly

They believe in God,
Even though
They don't see him.

Yet they don't believe in her pain
Because they can't see it.

Proof is what they seek
To believe,
Yet no amount of proof
Seems to satisfy them.

Aren't the shadowed smiles,
Distant eyes,
And fixed expressions enough proof?

Aren't the long sleeves,
Different beliefs,
And countless heaves of anguish enough proof?

Aren't the constant tears
And withdrawal from peers enough proof?

Yet all you've been doing
Is misconceive,
Assuming there is no grief.

Just because you can't see her pain
Doesn't mean she doesn't suffer
Just because she seems so bright
Doesn't mean tears have never
Flowed in rivers down her face.

Tossed

In the darkness
They tossed me
They left me there
For it to engulf me.

In the scorching heat
They tossed me
They left me there
For it to incinerate me.

In the ocean
They tossed me
They left me there
For it to swallow me.

At the back of their head
They tossed me
They left me there
To be forgotten.

Around paper corners
They tossed me
They never left me there
A memory never stayed.

Exact Opposite

Don't look at me
With an innocuous gaze,
I know all you are
Is a pretentious maze.

Don't play me,
I know all you do,
You instigate rumours
And spread tumours.

Don't fake sympathy
I've looked through the depths of your heart,
I know it's icebound
And all you can manage is apathy.

Liar, Liar

I thought you'd erase all the pain
Love me for who I am
And not for your gain.

I thought you'd fill the emptiness,
Build me with friendliness,
And I thought you'd hug me with a kiss.

What do you want from me,
Why'd you never shed your skin
And show the real you to me?

Why'd you commit this deadly sin?
Can't you see all of the change in me,
Can't you see that you've deranged me?

You used me,
Abused me,
All in the end
To exchange me.

The Hidden

Her mouth was open wide,
I didn't know if she was crying or laughing.

His wrist was pink,
I didn't know if he was bruised or kissed.

The dog smiled,
Given a slap or a nap.

The cat died,
The funeral held in the tide.

The frog killed,
And was tamed a hero.

The prince gone,
The only evidence a gun.

The teacher cried,
She's dying of cancer.

The student laughed,
He's whipped at home.

The butcher revived
With his last breath
The lonesome sheep
Died forever thanking the butcher.

The Holy

Kiss the clouds
Pluck the trees
And kill the birds

Lick the seas
Caress the winds
And drown the fish

Inhale the sun
Exhale the light
Steal the warmth

Stab the sky
Tear the horizon
Burn the lives

Battle the lilies
Assassinate the bees
And suffocate the souls

Look inside their eyes
And hear between their lines
There you will find the lies.

Let the holy live.

They Jumped

Problems with empty solutions
And solutions with fruitful problems.

A tear on her lashes,
With a hollow mouth
And a drowning throat
She smiled.

Cocaine in his nostrils,
With an empty body
And a bleeding heart
He laughed.

Liquor on her lips,
With a bruised soul
And a broken mind
She danced.

Heroin in his veins,
With a toxic relationship
And a hungry feeling
He kissed.

Ecstasy in her mouth.
With a greedy family
And a heartless society
She was quiet

Marijuana in his windpipe,
With abusive parents
And cruel teachers
He closed his eyes.

Darkness engulfing their system,
With empty solutions
And fruitful problems
They jumped.

You

Sometimes I forget you,
The smell of your thin t-shirt
The texture of your brown hair
The taste of your blue lips

And it's so cold
My feet burn
My blood freezes
My heart aches

Because all I taste is your venom
All I smell is your hatred
And all I see are lost souls
What did you to me?

Sometimes I remember you
What we didn't have
What we never had to lose
I can almost see it in your eyes

Spitting words
Tearing flesh
I got your blood between my teeth
Your breath between my lungs

Sometimes I forget you,
The smell of your t-shirt
The texture of your hair

The taste of your lips
Because all I taste is your venom
All I smell is hatred
And all I see are lost souls
Whatever did you do to me?

And it's so crowded
My eyes go blind
My hands go numb
My mind no longer mine

And I tear you apart
Because who really are you?

Adrift

Throw me in the ocean
In the arms of waves and bubbles

Leave me there to be
Adrift I close my eyes and count to three

With glassy eyes
I drown under the rise

Leave me be, I do not need you
I drift like the bird who flew

Who was left blind
When the stars aligned

The sky above, so clear and vacant
Emptied of love I disappear and chant

The salty residue is what I am
In all the areas, there's a part of me in every gram.

Oh, the View

My ashes under the soles of your feet
Mixed with your finest venom
Right under your control

You drink my blood
In your golden vodka flask
Cheers to you, cheers to you

My eyeball, your golf ball
Gently rolling on the grass
Of your blue backyard

My body, your stress toy
My freedom you tinker with
Because my soul is nothing but your lab rat

You cuff my hands, tie my feet
Under the bed you carve your initials
On your favourite stress toy

You feed me poison
The path to my deathbed
Blindfolded, I walk it, your foot just behind mine

You hold my hand
For the cheering crowd I bow
Your success, your victory

Nails digging into my back, I absorb the pain
The collar's too tight around my neck
My vision goes blurry

With your toxic words
Authority is yours
And you send me to the ocean

To swim amongst the sharks
And dance with the eels
In your bedroom tank

All for you to see
Oh the view, father
Oh the view.

Abused

Abused,
Constantly used,
Hit until she's bruised

Abused,
Yet always accused,
Always misused

There's magic in the air,
She was hit with words
But her heart never bruised.

The Truth Is...

I tape scary pictures on my wall
But I'm too scared to look at them,

I create friendly ghosts in my mind
But I'm too shy to associate with them,

I paint beautiful art on the ground
But I'm too blind to see it,

I cook tasty food in the house
But I'm too full to taste it,

I build strong buildings at school
But I'm too weak to keep them,

I give stacks of money to you
But I'm too poor to note it,

I wear stylish clothes all the time
But I'm too distracted to notice,

You always compliment me
But I'm too deaf to hear you,

You're always committing a crime
But I only see you as sublime,

I know you hurt me
But I'm too forgiving to admit it

And I am indeed infatuated in your skies
Because these constellations are so full of lies.

What I Had

I had a dream,
That my mother crushed
I had a kitten,
That my father tossed

I had a tear,
That my grandpa effaced
I had hope,
That my grandma killed

I had a hole,
That poetry filled
I had fear,
That music erased

She crushed my dream,
With her muscular words
He tossed my kitten,
To the oceans far away

He effaced my tear,
Beginning with my cheeks and ending with my lips
She killed my hope,
With her evil eyes

Poetry filled the hole I had,
With roses and violets
Music erased the fear I knew,
With golds and diamonds.

Welcome Here

Locked doors
And rusty throats

Lost kids
And heartless mothers

Dry lives
And obedient fathers

Sleepy eyes
And sharp knives

Fearful hearts
And taunting smiles

Salty tears
And laughing shadows

Doors locked with wax,
Kids lost in the night

Lives sucked of life,
Eyes left to reconstruct
Hearts drowned in death,
Tears gone with a breath.
Welcome here, come forth
Into the world where problems cease to exist.

A Pretty Girl

Shaking the hands of the dark
Making deals with the devil
Bow down to the ocean
Your sanity forever lost

A pretty girl
With bloody thoughts
An empty sky
With bright stars

A clear face
With runny mascara
A healthy soul
With a shredded heart

Singing with the winds
Colouring the tides
She lied
She lied

Carried by the clouds
To the underground
She died
She died.

Watch It Fade

The thoughts in my head aren't mine
Those marks are my teeth
That eye is yours
To get it back you must be refined,

Close your eyes
And beg to stay, through your lips I hear a sigh
Just drink your face
And eat your heart

Pour it into
The shimmering surface
Without a trace

Because
I feel alive when I'm asleep
And lost when I breathe.

The Colourful Future

I'm not ready
For the colourful future
The dark corners
And alien butterflies

To be set free
Is what I dread
Keep me caged
Behind the bushes
In your blue backyard

Keep me caged
Cuff my wings
And hold me tight
Because very rarely do you throw me into the clouds
Of your blue backyard

You see, I'm far from ready
And only if you can see,
Look behind you darling
I'm right here waiting

I'm not ready
So keep me protected
In the cages behind your eyelids
Of your blue backyard.

Love

You were a prisoner of the dark
So I pulled out my eyes
And gave them to you
To see the beauty and the pain
Of a life you so much hated

You were drowning
In a sea of your own confusion
So I ripped out my lungs
And gave them to you
So you could breathe

You were angry
And forever lost
So I sacrificed my body
Your canvas to protect
One that you never loved

I was hungry and dying
So I poured my love in a jar
And gave it to you
Forever to keep
To remember and to share

Because, my dear
How am I to live
With no body or a soul?

Up in heaven
I would stare
At the sorrow of your being
And the beauty of your life
With another love.

Monsters

Are these problems of life
Or monsters with a knife?

Will they slice
Or will they be nice?

Will they criticise
Or sympathise?

Will they shout and attack
Or will they stand back?

Are these problems
Or monsters?

Because I'm bound to you by a chain,
One that I just can't begin to explain.

The Work of Monsters

I could hear my heart pump,
My blood flow,

And suddenly,

The pain was escalating,
My body suffocating

Problems, from every direction, poking
Fingers, from all around, pointing

Dread creeped up my arm
Like an old friend
He said hello

Pecked me on the shoulder,
Left a scorched rose
And an icy feeling in my tummy
A trinket
He said, from me to you
A memory to forever see me through.

Father said don't you complain
Strong girls can handle the pain
Never should she crack, because from giving out secrets we must refrain
And then she was gone
Gone like the wind
And remembered like a story.

Paranoia

Is that a ghost I see?
Oh, it's merely a shadow
No, it mustn't be.

Are those footsteps I hear?
No, they're whispers
Voices of the dead
Oh, it's just my head,
Refusing to let go of thoughts that have fled
Thoughts which I must behead,

Is that a breath I felt on my shoulder?
No, it's just a breeze
More like a monstrous basilisk with pink disease.

Their Creation

They watched me,
Feeding off
My agony
And drinking my tears.

They dumped me
Into the river of excruciating pain
And endless hatred.

They ignored me,
My calls for help,
My pleas
I fell victim for a deadly disease.

Instinctively they claimed me
An outrageous monster
They fled away
I'm contagious, they left me to decay.

My blood
Was made of pain
And apathy
Ashamed, they looked down, for their inability to explain

In the end,
They blamed me
For the cold-hearted
Monster I've become.

They blamed me
For their creation.

Off to College

At 17, she told me to visit every weekend
At 18, she told me to talk to her through the entire bus ride
At 19, she told me to call her when I reach home
At 20, she told me to text her when I reach home
At 21, she said she'll be asleep, have a safe journey
At 22, it's been a year since I've heard from you
Can I still come visit?
What's your new number, mother?
Like your many fans, Snapchat is the only means for me to know you're alive
Where are you?
Spending the summer in Greece?
Off to Spain for the mid-year vacation?
Taking a month off in Mauritius?

Where are you mother,
What made you forget your eldest?

Ana

She has awoken
Beware, beware
Of her magic tricks
And her moans of despair

Eyes swallowed whole,
Hollow sockets with ghosts reaching out
Ghosts with a sugary smile and a sticky grasp

She is awake
Take care, take care
Of her silky lunacy
She has you under her stare

Jawline as bruised as can be
Collarbones crystal clear,
Ribcage outlined by a scarred layer of skin
Hip bones as sharp as a spear

Bony hands with a coppery scent
Split ends with the sorrow of life,
Burned toes and dripping nails
Fragile stick thighs

Hollow sockets
Sharp bones
Thigh gaps,
Ana's work is done here.

Shadows

Bitter tears
Invisible peers
Yes, I'm still sane

Hollow sockets
Shallow pockets
Yes, of course I'll live

A foggy brain
Some saggy cheeks
Just another girl at the creek

Smiley shadows
And shadowy smiles
Oh, just what a beautiful girl she is!

Sharp smiles
And bloody lips,
Haunted eyes
And silky voices,
Warm hands
And sticky grasps,
So many hungry shadows
With such welcoming faces.

Oh, just what a dark world she lives in.

Mommy

One, two, three
One beautiful girl under a tree
Only a few years old and she wishes to be set free

Poor mommy under this very soil
The days have stretched to months and I can't help but recoil
You told me it was only a nap when you rolled onto your other side

Till this day I sit and wait
To take revenge from this deadly breeze
That has stolen mommy and left her underground to freeze

Can you hear me when I pray for you
Can you feel it when I fall asleep right here for a day or two
Can you see me dig with this rusty screw?

Because today I depart
No better day than my own birthday
For me to find you if you have lost your way to me.

Addicted

Bloodshot eyes
And red-hot petals

Bloody livers
And flooded rivers

Clogged ears
And smoggy brains

Rusty rings
And filthy sharpeners

A dry oesophagus
Ready to occupy a sarcophagus

Leaving a shell that's been shed
To be buried

All this for an hour of euphoric floating.

Sleepless

It's a nightmare
I'm yet to wake up from
Sleep is the monster
Lurking behind tears
Luring you into a pit

I begged for victory
And that I was given,
I fell to the clouds
The grassy grounds have released me

My soul walked out for a stroll
Now it's lost,
Through heroin hills
Cocaine mountains
And whiskey rivers
It is nowhere to be found.

I feel it tugging at the pit of my stomach
The grounds urging me to sleep below
My insides whither and litter the floor
And here I sit, atop this roof
Watching the flowers down below, cherry blossoms turning to bushes
Autumn leaves my body sheds, yet I stand
Tall and high
Never to be felled by my own consent
So here I wait,
My permission you are granted
Do the honours, have the courage
Let me light the silent sky.

Fear

Maybe my mind is scared of the forest
Of the dancing lines
And dying lives

Maybe my heart is scared of the universe
Of the powerful tides
As they multiplied

Maybe my soul is scared of the fire
Of its power to incinerate
Leaving me in a drastic state

Maybe my body is scared of the stars
Of the dazzling dark
Distinguishing me with a mark

Because I'm scared of the truth
The one burned into your palm
Running through your veins
Empowering your being

The deadly truth has got me in its grip
No matter how much I pretend otherwise.

Failing is absolutely not an option
I will not cry, I am not weak
I don't want help, I will not speak
Although inside, I'm on the verge of breaking
But I will not cry, nor will I shriek
I'd rather erupt, because I am not weak.

Robotic

Charred skin
Chapped lips
And heroin slips

A red nose
Dead tissue
And cocaine rows

Yellow teeth
A blue tongue
And tobacco meals

No pain, no love
Because I'm only a robot
In human form
Living a human life
In a world full of robotic humans

I've never meant the hugs
The kisses
Or the love
I may be blind in the eyes
But I am not oblivious to your lies

From the ashes, watch my soul arise
IV lines,
Cracked ribs
And broken hips
Death is around the corner, sweetheart.

The Devil

Nails digging into her hips
Warmth choking her throat
Love pouring from your insides

Her blood, your pleasure
Her pleas, your motivation
Her yells, your joy
Her hopelessness…your strength

One time
Staining her memory
Perfuming the air
Swimming through her tears

A devil in you.

She was the survivor of an attack
She saw it in your eyes
All the things you lack
Using all her strength she tried to rise

With your bloody fingers
And your sweaty hands
With your cold eyes
And your deathly grip
She found the devil in you.

Listen

Plastic cake
And rubber juice
Be careful or you might trip over frozen cookies

Look up at the candy clouds
And suck gummy tongues
Be careful or you might fall into a milky river

Because He is pressing
Down on my chest
And suffocating me

He knows I can do it
No tears are allowed
Said the man in my dream

I'm breathing
Dancing leaves and feathers
But the air doesn't reach my tattered lungs

I'm talking
Cheerful melodies and lullabies
But the sound is trapped in my crushed throat

I'm reaching out
To the holy and the possessed
But everyone is so far away

My legs are chained to the ground
With milk and honey
And I can't move a limb

I get used in my dreams
And I get bruised through my life

I've been stolen of my soul
And I've been beaten to the ground

I was choked by rough hands
And I was slapped red all around

Demons have inhabited my mind
Angels dance through my blood
And you watch me from above

'Cause darling
I am just a sculptor
Sculpting horses on blood-red wrists

Plastic cake and rubber juice
Candy clouds and gummy tongues
Stolen souls and red tears

One conversation
Over and over
Many different voices

In the end
I'm six feet underground
Buried alive

It fucking hurts
But shhh said He
Because this is but a trivial accomplishment.

The Monsters Are Out

The monsters are out
They're out to play

Dancing in front of his eyes
And whispering behind his forehead

Perhaps a whiff of liquor on their breath
But definitely a deadly hunger in their eyes

Their bloody paws and sharp claws
Have left his face in a ghastly mess

Taunting the sick
And fooling the rich

Beware,
Beware

Because the monsters are out
They're out to play.

A Pair

Frizzy blue curls
Eyes of pearls,
An upturned jewel
With a smile that's cruel

Dim stars exposing her face,
She's part of the chase
Entrapped in her own mind

Strands of silver
Hiding eyes with a glitter,
A sharp sword
With a faint smirk

A creamy complexion,
With absolutely no direction
Entrapped in his own reflection

Together as one,
Apart as none
They gaze into the future to come.

It

It quenches my thirst
When I'm thirsty,

And cleanses my rusty thoughts

It fills my hunger
When I'm hungry,

Washes the problems,
The problems of yesterday,

And brighten the gifts,
The gifts of today.

Taking you
To another world,

A world of dreams
And wonders.

Glimmer

I break
The glimmer of radiant light falters
As I shatter to the ground

Cause I'm way too manipulative of a liar
In the depths of the darkness
I'm way too good at dispensing my energy

I give you a piece
I save him a part
I offer her a glimpse

I break
The glimmer of radiant light falters
As I shatter to the ground

Light fades, leaving me forever engulfed
Hope diminishes, saving me from the harshest fall
Candles die, then you leave

And I know I'm no good for you
On rooftops I chase
Because I am haunted

And I break
The glimmer of radiant light falters
As I forever shatter to the ground.

From the depths of my heart
Emerged a thorny rose

From the warmth of my smile
Radiated a love so manipulative

Scorpions, the masters of manipulation
For their own protection.

Oasis

To the beasts of my mind
I had confided
To the daggers of my heart
I had departed

I wandered in the darkness
Fluttering in the cold December chills
I was one lost soul
Walking the streets of insanity

Until a warmth grasped my hand
A warmth so beautiful, it had long hair
Hazel eyes
And a creamy complexion

It took me to the welcoming breezes of April
Then with one touch
I had landed in a euphoric limbo
That late December night was my oasis.

In a World of Abeyance

Now I'm fucked up
And I'm thrown out

In this vast world of abeyance
I met an angel

Who did things to me
That no one else did

And now I'm fucked up
I've been thrown out

Sulking in the streets
Don't want to talk about it

How could I've been so right about it
Not a thing to do about it

Things have been done to me
With no one else to see

I walk and walk
I'm lost, I beg

But it's too late
Because I'm fucked up
I've been thrown out and I'm on my own now.

Forlorn Pearl

In the depths of the sea
I am rejected

A forlorn pearl
Has been stolen from the love of her shell

Swallowed by waves
And tossed by currents

Once upon a time
Lay a pearl who's a victim of a crime

In between the grains of sand so deceptive
One shiny gem is held captive

By the love of all
She is suffocated

From her only love
She is rejected

Once upon a time
In the golden sand

Rejected and refused sat one forlorn pearl
At a loss in such a monstrous vacancy.

Exceptional

Stand aside
You're exceptional
And tell me what makes you so terrified

In the moonlight and twinkling stars
You sit quietly battling a silent fight
All encompassed in one crystal tear

Half goddess, half devil
Lost between good and evil
You master the act of deception except you're the only one who falls victim

Fooling your own perception
You sleepwalk right through the gates of oblivion
All the while your mind plays the soft tunes of a violin.

The moon focused on the sun
Wanting what's out of reach and beyond imagination
But only if she looked at the dazzling stars
Just right beside her
They kept her warm
Made sure she stood out in the gloomy skies of the night.

Quicksand

I hang from the sky
I'm chained to the ground
These problems
They're pulling me apart

Quicksand at my feet
All the way up to my chin
I'm swallowed whole
My sun-kissed fingers crossed behind my back

Volcanic eruptions raining from the sky
My hair, a fiery rage, the highlight of the night
My heart's ashes in the show's opening dance
That toxic breeze surrounds my corpse

One, two, three dollars for your share
Step forward
Get the experience of a lifetime
Come release this soul to the devils of heaven.

Speechless

I'd die for you to know
I need your help
At night I cry for your presence

In the periphery I find you
I make you laugh, I try to talk
How much I have inside and how very lost I am

I want you to know
But I never want to tell you
I want you to insist every time I refuse

I want you to ask even though I'm forever incapable of an answer
I want you to hold me despite the countless time I shout to be alone
I want you to sense the hurricane inside me

Because my lips are stitched
My tongue's been severed
And I can't utter a word

The shadows of the night
They held me in a corner, said let's celebrate
They gave me a kiss and my tongue was gone

The angels of the skies warned me of sinning
They said I'm better safe than sorry
Then helped me and stitched my mouth shut.

String of Insanity

This string of insanity in my brain
It grows and tangles
I'm at a loss as to what it feeds on

This string occupies my mind
It threatens to suffocate me
Says it'll choke me if I don't agree

My vision's blurred
My face feels furred
This string, it's killing me

The puppet of insanity
It carves a smile on my face
It pulls out all the lies

It puts on a show
I can't say no
Because my body no longer is mine.

Stone of Reality

This stone of reality
I hold onto
It's dragging me down into the deep waters

It promises me a world of wonders
A life of treasures
And a luxurious living

I try to let go
It's glued onto my hands
It pulls me down

It's dark and only getting darker
It's cold and getting colder
It's too late

This stone fights my string of insanity
A battle in my mind
A prolonged fight

One pulls me to the clouds
And the other drowns me in cold waters
An ongoing quarrel behind my eyes

The battle that no one knows of
In the morning they shout, at night they whisper
I'm forced to keep quiet about it.

Lost and Forgotten

I awake
Debris in my hair
Dirt in my eyes
Weeds intertwined between my fingers

I lie in the midst of fog
Surrounded by the chirping of crickets
I'm accompanied by one hungry crow
And insanity so scary in his eyes

To my right stands the Eiffel Tower
Tall and bold
To my left is one forgotten trolley
The tower of such a majestic crow

A bloody river flows and hisses
One hungry crow in between my legs
He leans down, gives me kisses
Nourishes the growing hunger in his body.

Older

Through the clouds of agitation
The shadows of desperation find their way to me
Such great ideas, they'd let me see

I turn the music up
I get lost in the waves
And try not to listen

I used to be confused
But now I know
I'm no longer the kid I used to be

Love is extraordinary
Rarely do loving families exist
I used to wonder why, it kept me up at night

I'd cry at night
I'd wish for an end to this fight
While my mother screamed in the kitchen

Little did I know
I'm just like her, she's just like me
We all die victims to the shadows of our minds.

Humble Hero

Drip, drip, drip
One big boy on a trip
His eagerness bit a bloody bubble on his lip

He was daring, he pushed the door
Ready to explore
Thinking he was ready for what's in store

Tick, tock…tick, tock
They gave him time to backtrack
His enthusiasm set a raging fire

Fire bites his fingers
It licks his smooth locks of hair
Gives him a memorable kiss on the neck

On and on he goes
Towards the source that houses all feelings
Towards the shadow king

One humble hero
His ashes stomped on by the upset trio
King, queen, and princess always win.

You see this anger I bottle up
Yes I let it surface
I feel it boil
I can smell the simmering surface of my insides
Fireworks go up inside
Red, green, blue
Fireworks pop, they go kaboom
I can hear them tear me apart
I sit here
Under this yellow tree
Life is hard
It never ever works
You just try your best not to get hurt
But sometimes it's better to let yourself go
I was just a kid back then
I'm still a kid up till now
I skip, I jog
I used to be mad
Not a thing changed till now
I let it hit me hard
I fantasise about the life beyond
I feel it's better to let me go
Let my soul flutter and fly far, far away
All the while fireworks light up my wings
So they make sure I fall deep down.

Sacred House

I'd never thought there'd be a tree
As tall as me
Always thought I'd see you there
To set me free
I didn't think I'd see these vines
Snake their way to my heart
Infiltrating my sacred house
They gave me no choice but to turn this home into a slaughterhouse.

She decided to free herself
Set her golden wings afire
And drift in between the purple valleys

Fumbling with rusty locks
To escape this box
So she lights a candle

In the warmth of the flame
She rocks herself
And closes her eyes

Taken to a faraway world
Where the birds always sing
The sun never hides

She opened her mouth
Let out a heartfelt melody
To rid herself of these heavy secrets.

Hands

My face feels hot
I can't open my eyes
My temples throb

Handkerchiefs cover your diamonds
Crystalline sharpness
And porcelain beauty

My arm feels numb
I can't move my hand
My fingers are sickly

Rosy knuckles
Precede such smooth fingers
What a pageant princess

My hands
They weave, knit, farm
And keep me alive under the scorching sun

Your hands
They're pampered, powdered, protected behind a velvet handkerchief
But they haven't served you once.

I've tried and tried
Day and night
To count these dying leaves
In this forest I call home

In the distance
I listen to waves crashing on the shore
In such harmony you can ask for no more
So, I sit back and admire the dark skies

One, two, three
I lose count of these dazzling stars
Following their instructions
But I never shine bright, because I do it all wrong.

It's like you gave me a new life
New me, new chances

A life where I could laugh
And one where you could love

You breathed life into my lungs
It all started with a touch of our tongues.

A lot of times I'd wish to touch you
But it's a mistake I can't afford
Because I'd rather have a flourishing rose behind the glass
Than a dying one at my fingertip.

Vessel

My mind's getting in the way
Can't feel what's going on around me
I reside in a cloud of confusion
Lost between the good and the bad
To my left I see the malnourished dying
To my right I see the thieves ruling the world
My friend dies
My family thrives
The world spins
Not in the least bit affected
I let out a sigh of despair
And I,
I can't move I am chained
In the midst of this blight
I'm always getting older
I do not know which is the safest way to go
I am sitting here
They whisper for me to play king
A thing I want nothing to do with
But it claws around my insides
It's trapped in my ribcage
I am forced to rule here
Through my eyes they see
And there isn't a thing I can do
Because I am the vessel for this parasite.

Poetry
Whispered the horror story
Of her life.

Whenever I close my eyes and listen close
You're no longer there in my heart.

Cigarette

I'm addicted to something I've never tried
This feeling it haunts me
Day and night
It never leaves me
The only thing I'm ever thinking about
It's got its hands on me
I'm suffocating
I can smell the nicotine all around
I can see the smoke, it engulfs me
I can taste it
I feel it
It's invisible, yet very powerful
A ghostly parasite that's took a hold of my dreams
I can't help but fall victim to the wonders of this rolled up paper
I ingest it, I inhale it, I swallow it
I take it all in and can never get enough of it
'Cause I'm so addicted to something I've never even tried.

In the silence of hope
My thoughts let out their invisible claws
And tore my dreams to shreds.

My parents chanted a mantra
My body obeyed
On and on
Two words
Day after day
Clueless of their intentions
Days stretched to months
I forever obeyed
Without a second thought.

I don't like this new life
This danger zone
You've thrown me in
I'm still too young
To understand how it works
I wish I could freeze the years
That have gone by
But I'd rather die
Than see the disappointment in your eyes.

Shelter me from the pain
Give me a home in between your arms
Make me feel like a princess
In your castle let me shine
Let me shine and glow
Like the diamond you say I am.

I hear it singing a lullaby
I glance
Then darkness engulfs me forever.

Poverty

Poverty, that sickly dementor
Our life it stole, leaving us no honour
Vivid dreams haunt the nights
Endless prayers go unheard
Rivers dried
The young have cried
Year after year, poverty strikes our hope.

The Voices

I hold a dagger
To carve my insides out
The voices said, the voices say
That there is no other way
Start at your weakest point
All the way up to your chest
Reach in, give in to this request
And grab this heart that's oppressed
The voices said, the voices say
They warn me to never disobey.

Music is the zephyr
That gives wings to my wingless thoughts
And life to my broken poetry.

Whispers

Whispers of voices and thoughts
Wishing for killer shots
Walking amidst the chaos
Watching little kids go rebellious
Warnings of mothers go unheard
Whispers of voices and thoughts
Whispers leaving my mind in knots.

Smile, smile
You expect me to run a mile
My heart in shreds all the while
I see you carve a princess
From this evil queen.

Wanderlust Mind

My mind starts to wander
What it does
Among hills of insanity, I wonder
Because my thoughts are over-thinking
And my stomach is in knots
But I mustn't ponder
With the ends yonder.

Tears, the crystal residue of your trapped soul.

Fragile Creation

She was the vocal cords of a nation
Such a fragile creation
Entrapped in the perplexity of leadership
Until one night
She was kidnapped and buried alive
Knock, knock
There was never life behind that lock.

Trapped in this mirage
Of my own creation
Where birds cry
Scattering the sky
With their loathsome truth
So I closed my eyes
And drew on the walls holding me captive.

*

In the depths of my fears and the folds of my life

My world indeed
Is a wingless Phoenix in need
Surrounded by the desire to always succeed
Surely your satisfaction is guaranteed

Your magnets have affected my idea of attraction
Origami in the air has led to my abstraction
Under the moon, within the droplets of rain, I can only picture your reaction.

This knife of grief
It tears my heart in shreds
The voices of doubt
Make me find pleasure in the crimson rivers.

I feel so lonely
Yet I'm never alone
Night and day
All I think of is the unknown
If I'll ever see my name engraved in stone
With but an inkling of hope in my tone.

I try helplessly
To hold onto hope
As my urges unfurl the rope

I try desperately
To swim through the sand
As my thoughts nibble on my flesh

But I fall
And then I drown
In my own ocean of dark regrets.

I sit on a chair, my golden throne
I promise I'm not on drugs
I ask my friend and he just shrugs
Like my red chandelier
You hang from the ceiling
Crimson blood dripping
That fury and the rage
They tell me to flip the page
Where there are no second chances
Where I am creative, arts and crafts
Scissors and knives
Saws and axes
A variety to choose from
So I can open you up
Uncover the secrets you hide
The love you conceal
Layer by layer
To find a heart encased in filth
The ashes of your attempts
You cry and yell
Such music to my ears
I hear you say the words I cannot speak
So I dig deeper and further
With the silver spoon
You gave me on my birthday, mother
I dig and dig
Trying to find the treasure you promised
Beyond your heart
Such work of art

On and on I go
Until what's left of you is but a hollow shell.

The Ghost Man

A few little boys
Making some noise
Just what the Ghost Man enjoys

Behind yellow trees
They fly their kite to God
So maybe He can hear their pleas

Under the burning sun
They yell and shout
But the Ghost Man pulls out a gun

The golden gun of their fears
The Ghost Man sneers
And shoots right through their dreams

It thundered and it rained
No longer a few little boys
Because of the Ghost Man's pains.

Vengeance

She's telling me to please eat
She's telling me to please vent
She's telling me to please sleep

They say they'll call my mother
Make sure this goes no further
So I don't swim too deep

I look down to my hands
They're on fire
From this burning desire

To meddle through their thoughts
To sew their fate in a vengeful pattern
Button eyes and smiley faces

Give them the pleasure of visualising the deep sea
To swim amidst the shadows and witness the chaos
Where thoughts whisper and the waters cackle

Hold my hand
Let me show you
Let your innocence be gone

Into the cold waters we dive
Don't you be afraid, little one
I'll keep you safe in my treasure box

In my treasure box
Under the grains of sand
I'll keep you safe behind all those locks.

Golden Light

I swim, from one country to the next
Across the pacific
My arms ache from paddling this canoe
In a sea where there are no islands I can see, but plenty that I can hear

My toes have died
From being in these cold waters that are blue
In the distance I see my crew
Enjoying the vibrant view

The need to vent
Leaves me dying to give you my consent
To rid me of this golden cent
But I can't repent

They need to see me stark
The flower that does not wilt
Drowning in an ocean of guilt
Which my thoughts have built

So I'm pictured
As a lion
King of the forest
Pastor of the church

Then you hold my hand
Begging me to give you a piece of my armour
This armour I've built
That encases my crying heart

And so I call the last at mind
The old tree which I have fallen from
But the tree only looks at me
You have put yourself in that sea
Only I can set myself free
Or drown trying

And just when the water's filling my lungs
I find the golden light and grasp it
I can feel it in my hand
Buzzing and burning

I can almost smell my flesh
Scarred and charred
I can almost hear the light
Have a peek, it whispered

I open my hand
To see what I have captured
But to my surprise there is nothing
Because there is no golden light in the depths of these blue waters.

Chess

It all started with a little boy who got fried
Then a few little boys on the street died
But not many people cried.

Why is it that we are blind?
What goes on through our mind
When we cannot even shed a tear for our own kind?

What drives our will to kill?
Hungry for a pint of blood to spill
With nothing to offer the dead but a daffodil.

This life, our own game of chess
Where, day after day, we seek success
But who are we trying to impress?

The lights illuminated a sky so sad
Poured warmth into a big, big city
With many, many people that wish to be pretty
Who keep their dead in cases
For the museum with an ocean of faces
And I'm scared of drowning
In a sea of sins
Where everyone's frowning
Over their stolen wins.

These tears you see
Are but the residue of thunderstorms
The reflection of a key
To the lock in me.

I do not like it when I'm sad inside
When my emotions are forced on a rollercoaster ride
I do not remember when my heart last cried
I want to shed this forlorn flesh
So I'm no longer a prisoner in this mesh
Life holds me captive
These thoughts are my guards
My feelings are my deceptive lawyers.

Abattoir

You are the vibrant star
In a world so bizarre
I fear one day you'll be a fragrant scar
In this memory that I glance at from afar
Do not leave Phoenix in this abattoir.

Creativity spilled on the parchment
As the golden quill danced
And her thoughts advanced

A princess was born
In a village so forlorn
And all the quill did was mourn.

The thoughts in my head
They spoke
Velvety words weaved into sinister actions
A silver hand caressed my cheek
A hoarse voice says it has something I seek
The shimmering folds of golden hair
Brush against this filthy air
Below this cliff
In the black abyss
There's someone waiting for my kiss.

Crimson Rivers

My eyes stared into the dark pool of secrets
I watched my hands
Crawl to my throat
I listened to my mind
Where there was a parade
Celebrating the solitude from which I was afraid
The voices of the past
Cheered the thoughts into action
Crimson rivers trickled down my fingers
A whiff of metallic scent tickled my senses
I ached for more
So harder I squeezed and deeper I went
And there I sat atop this stump
Puzzled and down
And so very lost
As to why my body is crying crimson rivers.

Stars

Look at the stars
As they shine above
Almost like a face

A memory you've stitched
Right before bedtime
One that you've bewitched

In your lap
The truth stains
Never will you quit

Your hands
Splintered and bruised
From all the ropes you've been trying

By your bed
A bloody scythe
Your partner in crime

In your head
A little girl
Won't stop screaming

A little boy
Won't stop crying
He stopped trying

And the doorbell rings
At this late hour
Who does life bring?

June

It is the month of June
When the sun wins over the moon
And the birds sing till noon
Along with the kids yelling all afternoon
In this sunny month of June.

Thread

One, two, three
A teardrop from a sea
It blurred her vision
Showed her clouds of red from the tiny incision

She closed her eyes
And practiced the lies
On and on
They ring in her head

At a loss of what she's done
Now she's left on her own
With broken promises from everyone
She writes down what needs to be said

For what holds her to this world is but a thread
Red in colour and weaved with dread
Broken promises killed the chord
Left alone, it bled until the girl dropped dead.

A witness to your pain
A power I never wished to gain
Scarlet tears of joy
Grow the flower that's meant to destroy
You hold my hand throughout
To push me in, no doubt
Underneath the flower's skin
I cry and plea forgiveness for this sin.

Indelible Kiss

There's an ice cream bucket inside of me
It's filled with icy water
In the midst of which eels are slithering
I can hear the crackle of their power
The smell of simmering hope
As my borrowed life slowly runs out
And I am now nothing but the bitter residue of sadness
For the eels have scarred me with an indelible kiss.

In your eyes, a galaxy shined bright
Swimming in an ocean of sorrows
As your body dazzled with a multitude of scars
Never have I seen such dull stars shy away from delight.

Grey

I'd like to perish and depart
A million butterflies
Grey in colour

But your face grows paler
As, in the sky, you see me scatter
And late at night, when you lament

Hold this grey rose to your lips
To remember my fading scent
Clutch this parchment to your heart

This is not the end but is the start
For you and I shall never part
Think outside the box, you are smart

Close your eyes
As this rose dies
Because in your dormant memories I await.

I'm trying
I swear I'm trying
Yet I always feel like crying
But my tears, I think they're drying
It makes me feel like I'm dying
I just can't help but keep on lying
Why are they so blind?
I'm a prisoner to this imagination, it's all in my mind
These lies, they aren't identifying
On me they say they're relying
Little do they know,
I'm eager for what awaits me below
What it has to show
So one foot's off the cliff and I am falling.

My body shivers in the night-time
The memories haunt me
Being a victim to your crime

A morbid fear
Comes visiting year after year
It clouds my vision, my mind is anything but clear

A beautifully quilted blanket of memories
Plays on and on
I think the only crime is this dreadful cycle in my head

My mind may have tricked my eyes
Not once did I question all these beautiful lies
It shook me like a surprise so grand in size

Caught me on a day so sunny
While I was in the background licking honey
And only then did I question reality.

Every Gloomy Midnight

Pale and scrawny was this redhead
Bloodshot eyes from the lack of sleep
A ginger ringlet hides his brows
As he twiddles with a thread
Red sneakers to match the lies of his eyes
Desolate thoughts stranded in a chaotic mind
Every gloomy midnight
An offering he must give with sheer delight
As the moon shies behind cloudy skies
A part of Jacob is sacrificed
He solemnly watches as it dies
Every night which lacks of hopeful light
He wraps this silky string tight
Until he hears the satisfying plop
Of another finger
On his wooden floor, he watches it drop
Every gloomy midnight.

A Malicious Gift

A whisper of your presence still lingers in the dark corners of my mind
A flicker of your soul still makes my mouth water
Your beautiful words echo in my head
Bouncing back and forth against these needy thoughts
They make me shudder

Although, your touch sweetens my tears
Your voice now is the fear I crave
In a dreamless land
I am your slave to sculpt
A gushing wound sprinkled in salt

The face I used to savour
Like porcelain I see it shatter
Seeping through my fingers, your shimmering flow of golden waves

And in the early morning my mind itches
From the sleepless hours spent trying to sketch the same you in my head
The you I never seemed to see through.

Warrior

The glint of a warrior in her fractured soul
The sharpness of a sword to her worn out edges
Her claws carve a sudden surprise
A pain beautified with lies
One, two, three
How glorious is she
Open your eyes
To her tormented cries
Just grab that key
One in a million, in this vast blue sea
To set this insanity free.

The velvety memories of our friendship
How through your fingers you let it slip
Drip, drop, drip
She bled a tear for every blow and hit
A sodden quilt she would knit
'Cause every night you'd pay a visit
And give her a kiss
Just another of a million kisses in this abyss
To cherish and remember this trip
The velvety memories of your friendship.

Cassidy

A heavy wave of depression
Carried by distant laughter
From all the people in the procession

It stings my wounds
And awakens the flutter of a kaleidoscope
They gather and beg me to hold onto the rope

Whispering a silent melody
Of a hopeful angel named Cassidy
Who could harm anyone with her toxic charm

Under my fingernails they say she lives
In my head I hear she never forgives
On and on she talks about the coming storm

Behind my eyes she is carving
Every time I listen, she is laughing
Whenever I ask, she says she's starving

I see across my eyes wisps of smoke
From every agonising brush and stroke
As she severs this rope of hope

She tells a tale of the coming storm
In which the skies are black
And the grounds are caved in, never to rise.

What was once a luxury,
Became in its most luxurious form a necessity.

Love of Hatred

Tears burned a silky trail
Once fair cheeks have now gone pale
A volcanic eruption
In a world known for its corruption

A once graceful deer
Now so full of fear
Galloping in the grey winds
Of the destruction of its only home

So she put her hand on her neck
Feeling the air go in and out
Seeing her chest go up and down
And squeezed so hungrily.

I like how silently the water sparkles
Under the sun, how gracefully it flows
The fiery forest, in my chest it crackles
Whispers of a wave, a domicile for a secret so grave
It flutters with every gasp for breath, threatening to explode
To the whole world it begs to be showed
Of all the wishes that must be told
One wish after another, my life it goes
I wish to be strong
To drown amidst the tanning models
All while I smile
I wish to be tough
Having my heart wither in this fire, it's had enough
I wish to be independent
Coughing up my own blood
I don't want to need a defendant.

I wonder why
For our oppressors we cry
They shed our skin, burn all the hope from within
But for them we would, without a doubt, die

How beautifully our backs they decorate
The shades of red and purple we must appreciate
Because only through them, shall we be great

Delicate fingers spider at the back of our heads
Pulling and tying lonely threads
Plucking the brightest memories, lest the joy spreads

A callous mess, our feet
From all the redemption we seek
Back and forth we go until this life is complete.

Icy trickles between my toes
Unexplainable love to a thorny rose
In a dark room I feel exposed

Whispers of a terrifying breeze
The hushed rustle of autumn leaves
My courageous Mary flees

To this wicked world
My every secret seems to be unfurled
Leaving me exposed, amidst the autumn leaves, they have all curled

A bony body adorns expressive art
The stories of a century forever a mystery
Flaming to explode in every star's history.

Burning trickles down his throat
Sweet tears as he wrote
In the dead of night, the cursive note

Insidious words
Stem from unknown worlds
Snake their way through this innocuous plea

The moon liquified in her eyes
Laughing in his arms, oblivious to all the lies
He was her prize in disguise

Her utmost pleasure he would guarantee
Her heart he had won
In this obsessed mind of his, all the fun had begun

A silver glint under her dress
With closed eyes, she's forced to acquiesce
Between her thighs she feels a caress

Her throat feels dry
As in the sky, birds cry
She's left under a tree to die.

Swan

In the dark of night and the light of day
My ferocious pencil is forever here to stay
From a tattooist in the dark of dawn
A lover is drawn
On the silky feathers of a beautiful swan
In the middle of this miserable pond
A story is scorched in the eyes of a fawn
From a vibrant heart
To a hole that's art
Comes a lively pain
Calling from the depths of the black waters
A heavy weight closing my eyelids
A basket full of orchids
In my palm, its thorns tattoo a rose only I can see
Their scent pleases me so intoxicatingly
The sticky petals of an orchid so magical
Amidst the beautiful pain, where the pencil stings a swan that sings.

Marathon

Tick, tock
The clock turns the lock
To my thoughts, I'm forced to listen
Behind my eyes I take a walk

Orange, yellow, and green
These leaves in my mind scream
Sharp feathers in this bloody stream

Tracking numbers, I hold the key
I've won the marathon
In this stream has it gone?

Inside my head
The leaves, they scream
Never will I win this race

Under my scalp
The gremlins count
The feathers shed and the leaves dead

To build a house they cannot see
With the feathers shedding
They are blind for eternity.

Obsession

The withered scraps of success
And the dew drops of toxic desire
Gasoline to this raging fire

The sliver of liquid silver
Drives this greedy obsession
Which needs no form of confession

The velvety ribbons of failure
Caress my heart after defeat's abuse
Squeezing it for fresh cranberry juice

Life to the flightless birds
Giving rise to triumphant words
Thoughts left undeterred

Scars coalesce with stars
My sight is blurred
Is it this that you would have preferred?

The salt in my blood
Stings my blind eyes
The fire in my heart
Burns my expired lungs
The metal in my claws
It scratches all my flaws
One by one I break each law
The inner morals of pride and dignity
Have gone to waste, a result of this blind-ended insanity
The euphoric sweet success
Drips from quivering lips
Onto these white sheets
Marking them with a lovely kiss
To the eager recipient
An address for lovers gone
Soldiers drawn
We belatedly yawn
Never to return, the flawed are gone.

Purple, red, and green
Screaming melodies, singing tragedies, and everything in between
Pumped from a lovely machine

In these veins
Swim notes and pains
In my head, she just complains

In the distance, a river calls
Listen as each wave falls
Behind palm trees, a monster crawls

She, cold and slick
Presses against my neck
Such rosy lips

Slowly bite into my flesh
Gently licks at my veins
Gives me a kiss

A once fair neck
I beg for more,
Now a tattered wreck

Behind closed eyes
I swim in this beautiful abyss
Never to be dismissed.

Golden fury at fingertips
Cover your eyes from this angry eclipse
In one, two, three my heart is ripped
The deadly secret, from my lips it slipped
Lust, from my tongue it dripped
In a pool of desire it flourished
Red in colour, lavender in scent
The wafts of such love
She couldn't help but lament
For her lost curiosity, she would repent
Beneath warm toes, a crystal river waves
From sad eyes, guilt flows
In the sky, stars twinkle
In this river, a diamond glows.

Rusty Hinge

Eyelids opened
In a field of daisies reddened
From this dreadful act,
Behind willow trees, a door creaks
One little baby squeaks
Skies cry rain
For this baby in pain
As this rusty hinge
Feeds coppery water
Into a mouth, which to life clings.

Defenceless Armor

Rusted artillery
From the salted tears of a hopeless memory
Encased in defensive shields
Yet to the law
Are defenceless
In the dullest of mornings
Scorched the sun and cried the birds
In the gloomiest of mornings
Tightened the ropes and died the girls
In front of rows of men
Loyal at the mind since ten
But traitors to this country at the heart again and again
With lovely mothers
Loved daughters and sisters
One by one robbed of oxygen
Lifeless displayed in front of the crowd
A crowd of knights in shining armour
But defenceless to a wicked law.

In the centre
A pool of a thousand stars
Encased by the love
Of a hundred dolphins
Enlightened by the fire of desire
It only flows through the tears of a liar.

Wounded and round
The place where not a soul drowned
For what is an eyeball
Other than a silent fountain?

Being Close

How does one get closer,
Is being close just names and pictures
Or is being close late-night talks and midnight walks?
Being close, being close
People in the ground, butterflies in the sky yearn for it
A different language to each person
Unique, a different feeling in their heart
A different colour in their mind
Butterflies in the stomach, may be worms for someone else.

How does one know it's fake
Leaving one with nothing but heartache
How does one know it's fake and not real?

A Wall Missing a Brick

Sometimes, dear times
The pain, I'd wish for it to compress together
Invisibly materialise and form a spear
Pierce through my weak chest
Go deeper into this heaving mess

Intangible, invisible
The pain itself
Forever untouchable

No longer a blue aura
Or a moist atmosphere
Rather a craving
So strong it is, they fear

Overwhelming the senses, it comes together as one
Strong and thick,
Kisses the middle of this gasping chest

Steals a breath
Gives you a glimpse of death
And cleanly
Comes right out the back

This wall of mine
Made of flesh so crystalline
Held high by a withered spine
Through your work watch it shine

For what is this chest of mine
But a wall
Missing just one brick

Come close
Caress this puncture you have made
Look through it, and tell me, who will have stayed?

Debris scattered on the ground
Days turn into weeks
Not a sound do you make

It's not that you're scared
Not that you're unable, but ashamed
Of such weakness, you'd hate to be named

Nights pass, days stretch
A lonely boy in the sky, you sketch
All the problems, all the faults

To anything else, you are blind
You wish, at the end of this race, wait your kind
Satisfaction you wish to find

Days turn into weeks,
Debris scattered on the ground
With your heart in shreds, you frowned

From this weakness you're ashamed
All your flaws you blamed
Your mind, I'm afraid will burn in flames

End this race
There's no better time or place
Be the winner in your case.

Mingled with threads of expectation
Young and at a loss towards communication

Thoughts at battle
Rebelling with actions, never once did he prattle
Under the limitations of obfuscation, he was
Trained to solve and forever evolve
Understanding the misunderstood, he was the falcon in a sky of jays.

Thieves

Rosy nails bleed
Black ink they leak
Scratched on dried leaves
The stories of thieves
How on a village they cast nothing but grief
As the sun rose and the sun set
Wealthier they got, without an inkling of regret
As, one by one, their needs demanded more
They weren't seen as mighty as before
For they jailed themselves in desire and greed
They spent the rest of their lives, never asking to be freed.

Violin

Overdosed on iron
The sweet metallic tinge
The rusty coppery scent
As down her throat it takes its descent

Every morning she operates on a hinge
With all her strength she'd push
Alone she'd steal a lick or two
In her room, she takes the shavings from her shoe

Overdosed on iron
On cloud nine she plays the violin
Her claws string a beautiful tune
From her veins, under a dark blue moon

Breathing life into the skies
The sweet metallic tinge
The rusty coppery scent
Running down her arm.

Gum-Covered Tarmac

Rainy nights
And gloomy days
Of what once was a happy ending
She writes

Footsteps in sync
Hands intertwined holding a drink
Between their thoughts there is a link
Her name on a bench, he had inked

Days stretched into weeks
Fires burned into embers
His voice, she hardly remembers
Love scorched his heart, but of that he never speaks

Under a blue sun
Gazing through hazel ringlets
What used to be their favourite field of daisies
Now a gum-covered tarmac

She writes
Through rainy nights
And gloomy days
What should have been their happy ending.

Painkillers

Taking painkillers
For the foggy mist in my brain
Free refills
Popping them one after the other

The singsong swish of knives no longer a bother
Ivory hills promise a field of pills
Here comes blue, my pain it kills
There goes red, my anger it defies
One yellow a day, to keep me from spreading lies

On the other side, the train I always see
Very fast it goes
Full of fury it chases my last red rose

Tremors of terror
Fear of making a single error
Crimson trickles decorate this wearer

As the train I always see
Very fast it comes
Colliding with this powdery chest
Sending me into a blue sky, I'm free

Kissed and caressed
By the foggy mist
I'm free to rest.

Sober

Buzzing tongue
Burning gums
And alert eyes

Foot taps on the ground
Fingers dancing in my lap
Waiting for the crowd to clap

The audience in my head
They cheer and smile
For me to be dead

Lonely nights
Spent in alleyways
I reek of liquor

No, officer, I'm not intoxicated
I can explain it, listen, it's complicated
I drunkenly drive, I'm alone, I'm isolated

Early mornings
Before birds set out with their warnings
I'm euphoric, I'm beginning the endings

Of course, officer, I'm sober
For my family, I'm never high
My mouth and eyes, they're just naturally dry

The audience in my head
They cheer and smile
For me to be dead.

Fourteenth of February

Calloused fingers caress angelic beauty
The edges and corners
All of the promising features

Running out of toxins
He'll now never be the same sinner
Days pass by, she gets thinner

Mist in the late-night air
Under these wooden stairs
Cheeks feverishly buzzing against the cold

Lips numb and tingling
Fingers rough and searching
The last ounces of an angel, seem so intangible

Lustful lips against cold blue ones
A masculine figure hovering over the remains of an angel
Hands press and embrace, such futile attempts to bring what once was

On the misty night of the fourteenth of February
A lonely man was very merry
He was, under the stairs, with a dying angel who wasn't imaginary.

Clueless Bird

The moon dies
It's a beautiful sunrise
His wings unfurl
Exposing in his chest a beating pearl

The skies cry
Now the devils fly
Around a clueless bird
Through tears, his vision is blurred

Be down with it
Shrieked one greedy devil
Around my throat, the pearl let it be
Bring him forth, a frail chest I shall slit

An exquisite feathered bracelet upon my wrist
Be down with it
Screeched one handsome prince
For gods and frauds shan't coexist

So down it went
Gone was the life ahead it hadn't spent
That frail chest was neatly slit
Beautiful feathers quietly plucked.

Sprinkle

Twinkle, twinkle
Rang the doorbell
It's my daily dose of sprinkle

Birds chirp
We will never know
They come in the mornings with their warnings

Twinkle, twinkle
Urged the fairy
It's your daily dose of sprinkle

Close your eyes darling
Inhale this
Do you feel the bliss?

Burning my skin, orange bubbles
Every day, the dose only doubles
A split second, I only seem to have all the troubles

Hidden under her quilt
All I feel is guilt
Lovely sprinkles, I can't seem to accept

Alone under the moonlight
Birds nowhere to be heard, I'm left without a hint
Of the orange kisses, I catch sight

They burn into my skin
Every night, one for every sin
Leaving me a victim from within

Twinkle, twinkle
Rang my fickle fairy
The daily spray of sprinkle

Sprinkle, sprinkle
Close your eyes
It'll only tickle.

Sad Place

The world is a sad place
Did you know?
Do you see?
On that building there's a crow
He drops dead in one, two, three

Why do we sleep?
Do you think we're weak?
Maybe we are,
Of ambiguity we reek

Maybe you're afraid
Of all the mysteries that unfold
Of all the secrets that you keep
Why do you sleep?

Can you hear?
Gallops of fear
In every corner, all around this atmosphere
There never was, there is no race
The world was always just a sad place.

Impress

The music screeches in my ears
It itches my brain and makes it bleed tears
My throat overfills, it's clogged
I feel trapped in my body

In a dark alley we take destructive turns
Until my nose burns
In a chaotic world of oblivion and desire
Layer by layer, I peel this skin
To feed the raging fire from within

Deep down I feel a flutter
And from behind I hear it whisper
Lights flicker under these ribs
I scratch and claw for them to grow brighter

Rhythmic thuds in my head
It's like I've hit it hard in a mental fall
Blurry eyes see a convoluted mess
I can't focus, I fight to impress

I grasp and pull
At the gushing light from my middle
I claw and scratch
But this greed, I just can't seem to snatch.

Incision

She tugged my shirt
She said come here
Let me tell you a secret
Cherry lips against ears so alert
I want to die for a year, she winked

Hold this red string, it pulsates
Once in a while it drips
That's when you take one or two sips
You'll feel that from life you've been ripped

Jagged nails stroked my back
Up and down
Back and forth
She tickled my neck

Scribbled a letter
In my favourite colour she pierced my chest
I asked her why
Did something happen?

She looked into my eyes
Said midnight happened
The door was closed
And in my own body I was a guest

My shadow was so distant
Fear and muffled breaths clouded my vision
In my belly they made a beautiful incision
And from then, I was always non-existent.

Flute

Under the moonlight
Amidst the gazing stars
Night after night
A ceramic flute is played

Whispering singsongs
Lulling the sleeping helpless
Out from the end came an orange light
To warm the birds in such a chilly night

Moist brings from hours of rain
Separated from scarred skin through years of pain
Tears crept down sunken cheeks
One after another, they raced to the bottom

Lee huffed and puffed
Aggressively vigorous
Pouring out the forgotten and buried
To sleeping birds

Once an orange light
Now a blazing sun
Fiery and ferocious
From the depths of a sad flute

Why won't life reverse the power

How can one stand and not cower

Stitches are tearing apart

What you have mended can no longer be called a heart.

Morse Code

One tap, followed by two then three
Morse code of the midnight anxiety
In a cold blue era
You're left alone without a hero

One tap, two, but not three
Blackened cheeks from mascara
Obsessive connections redden wrists
Blind compulsions we no longer resist

One tap followed by none
Futile calls unheard
Clouded minds create a gun
On lonely grounds, cries a bird

No tap, not two nor three
Head exploded into a hundred pieces
Blood and tears filled all the places
On lonely grounds, dies a bird.

Stars twinkled in a dark sky
Will you sing me a lullaby?
Shimmering strands in between calloused fingers

One lock loops over another
Daisies intertwined
Midnight kisses in bed

A silver dagger on a golden tray
Blistered fingers encase smooth steel
Crimson droplets, his work's pay
Close your eyes in one, two, three
Speak of this to nobody

Gloomy clouds suppressed sunshine
Hands behind my back
Tied strings of vine

Dirty nails caressed a fair neck
Glazed eyes, windows to a destructive wreck
Chapped lips whispered in my ear

He said, hush little girl don't cry
Pushed me over the cliff
Fly, angel, fly
Now I'll sing you a lullaby.

Algorithm

Encircled by the golden ring
Of euphoric rhythms that always sing
Governed by pattern, driven by envy
Amidst raging waves
Enlisting all that the soul craves

Legs shuffle, hands clap
On water surfaces slap
Echoes directed at the sky
Fury shadows pulsating at necks
Anger tremors seen in hands
Malicious envy wisps back and forth
The glimpses of a blackened heart

Legs shuffle
Hands clap
Water surfaces slapped
Eyes greened with rivalry
Surrounded by a lone swan
Urged to proceed within the depths

Euphoric rhythms
A part of this algorithm
Urged a swan to dive deep
Where no treasures sleep.

Infection

Golden tulips
Petals flourished at fingertips
Silky dew drips from drunken lips

Tulips now ashes
Petals caught in a breeze
Silky memories of drunken dew

A velvety connection
In the depths of my heart, maybe an infection
Shimmering the brightest of hues

Fallen tulips
Cracked lips
There never was a connection
It was only an infection.

The Heartbroken

Silly girl, silly girl
You know better
Than to run after the heartbroken

Little pearl, little pearl
Give him back his sweater
From his lips only lies were ever spoken.

Watch as feelings coalesce and lies unfurl
Suns set and moons rise
Hours stretch between his replies

The art grows bitter
Tears now salty
But in your heart,
He resides until one dies.

My heart beats to every dewy smile
My brain yells it's but a beautiful guile

My pulse quickens to every deep goodnight
My brain whispers to listen and be quiet

My heart aches in his gloomy absence
His brain smiles in colourful triumph

In his chest
A hearty celebration
To every beautiful prey in this operation

Velvety lies
Smooth and delicious
Unfurl at such wicked lips

Greed and lust
Grow and prosper
Behind a curtain of midnight lashes

Oh, blue waters
Teach my brain to hate
The person my heart holds dearest.

Paper-Cut to the Mind

From the embers of destruction
Have risen the smokes of creation
Obfuscation stutters at the sight of damnation

Bleeding thoughts trickle down
From the curves and crevices
Clarity stammers at the sound of loss

Raining down the problems of tomorrow
Bathing in yesterday's regrets
Infidelity shivers at the towering honesty

Colourful outbursts of euphoric hatred
Galaxies oozed from a paper-cut
To the mind of one smart kid.

Walls

Cracked with anger
Hollowed by the memories of decades
Papery to the touch
Splintered at the edge

To human secrets they have surrendered
For the broken they are the only shade
Alone at night, to your tears a witness
But to your protection they pledge

In between bricks
Sleeps the deepest sadness
When everyone accuses you of madness
Walls pledge to your protection.

Fat raindrops from heavens above
Caress the broken from the hells of below
In an ocean of fires
Floats a kitten on a tattered shoe
A far away breeze, its only clue

Amidst the dying crops
One felled scarecrow
Between its teeth, a hint or two
His head topped with a dusty hat
With nothing to offer but shade for an old cat

South and east coalesce
Under the ground a rat is tamed
Under the sun, a kiss is framed
On a chipped, red brick

Night is falling
God starts calling
Hummingbird's stalling
A guitar with a broken string
For Him, is no right offering.

Destruction

The sun awoke a little late today
The moon's gloominess has such a cold longing
Grass stained yellow from years of madness

A chipped chalk
Undecidedly rolls
The endless debate between a girl's scrawny hand
Or under a man's shoe

Sandy lashes hurt the eyes they're meant to shield
A throbbing head brings a glistening colour to concrete
Droplets shimmer and decorate sad grounds

Smoke in the air dances to freedom
Fires afar rage to revenge
Droplets shimmer and glisten
To euphoric destruction.

Pretty

Diamonds, crystal clear
Sharp as a spear
Against flamed red cheeks
And sad blue eyes

I guess this is what it feels like
To be pretty

Gold encrusted eyelids
Chipped at the edges
Flaky at the corners
Fall into tear-rimmed eyes

They say this is what it feels like
To be pretty

Bloodstained claws
Stroke paper-thin skin
Beautifully decorated with a rainbow
Purple lips, the gate to an intoxicated vessel

I know this is what it feels like to be pretty.

It's nearly 2 AM
The owls out give a watchful eye
My lower back itches
Seems too far to be reached
Perhaps a galaxy away
My legs are freezing
My palms are sweating
There's an eyelash swimming in my eye
Oh what an irritating thing
That song's been on repeat
For a few hours now
Or maybe even a few days
God, my shoulder aches
My body seems too heavy to lift though
Oh my, I forgot the faucet on
Dear lord, look the sink's overflowing
Look at those water droplets encroach
To the velvet bedroom carpet
Well, what a waste that is now
There I lay, as if a lifeless form
My throat is parched
Well, I suppose until the soaking carpet nears me
Wait is that a bird out I hear?
What a movie this mind plays on me
It's a knock at my bedroom door
There goes my night, a waste
It's a new day
Maybe a new year
Whatever is the difference?

Droplet from Hell

Autumn leaves with their sharpened edges
Cripple under footfalls
Slicing and claiming a trespasser for eternity

Crisp weather in a foggy cloak
All your cracked edges, it shall stroke
Bruises worn and adored, for they are your new robe

A fiery witness, radiating brutality
Raging the memories, igniting the wounds
For what is the sun, if not a droplet from hell?

Seed

Heart flip flops in a flutter
What a cluster and a racket
Such enclosed darkness is

Veins sputter and throb
Out in the cold open
The torn and worn-out ends

Raspy chest heaves
Up and down
Pushing against the pain

There's a ringing in the ears
Warning of nails that bleed
Because in your head there's an ingrained seed
And nails scratch both spheres.

Film on Repeat

It's so hot in here
The AC remote, it couldn't be nearer
But my arm, it's just not under my control

I can't stop humming
To this song, I don't even know
Something no part of me has ever heard before

Just a shimmer of life
Under dusty eyelids
Like a sound that's radiating through the waves of decades

I'm unaware of what I see
It's like a film on repeat
Day after day, the same beat

But my eyes have been robbed of sight
My mind can no longer comprehend
The thirst in my throat, it's nearly tipping me over the edge

It's all a film on repeat
The arm I can't control
And the sight I can't find.

Burning Stone

An ignited coal
Radiating the warmth of love
Emitting light from deep cracks

Grasped in soft palms
Once rosy and vibrant
Now a chipped mess

Love trickles in between the crevices
A burning stone held tighter
I can't let go of this hazardous love

Skies mourn above,
Breathe in a euphoric toxicity
Bleed out youth and all its eccentricity.

The taste of your lips
Still lingers in my mind
Your tears still
And forever will stain my fingertips
The shadow of your smile
Haunts my sleepless eyes.

Unified buzzes of an airy breeze
Horrific gazes, not much left till thy freeze
Powdery dust
An unforgotten scent at fingertips
Beams of hope, in past days dignity
Shot up straight, in the airy breeze
Hopeful for what once was
An unforgotten scent.

Fighter

Hold me when I'm frightened
Kiss me, my chest against my heart is tightened
Heart's fluttering
Tears whispering
The fire in my head flares brighter
This girl is no longer a fighter.

Companion

My little companion
Flutters its wings, content
Stings my nose with a kiss
A trace of pink follows its trail
On my fingers, I see each detail
It floats in a cloud around my head
It bobs its head when I've been misled.

And come nightfall
My companion kisses my eyes goodnight
With its tiny legs walking
Over the goosebumps on my lonely skin
Giving each a kiss
It tells me it's taking all the pain from within.

But come morning, the sun shines so bright
My body glowing in red
My little companion gives me a kiss
It flutters away.

The slushing of waves
Shushing a crying soul
The sky snowed in
Water swelled with grief

A lonesome almond rocked
Amidst the lives at sea
Braided wires clanking
The motor succumbs to no longer be
In such a bright night

The slushing of waves
A bright starless sky
A witness to waters enslaved

For there is no strangeness
In amorphous snow covering the sky
And dead grass blanketing the sea
To a crying soul.

Masks

Hands tremble in a midnight breeze
Voices echo in low degrees
The floorboards in our head groan
A film of dust showing no footprints
A ripple in time with no knock at the door.

We are the poor who live in luxurious homes
Bedazzled with gold and gemstones
Dinner served with piano tunes
Sleeping on feathered pillows

We are the poor with lonely afternoons
And a new doorbell which never sings
With walls harbouring unspoken words
For our floors see no guests

Living in a world using a global language of connectivity
Of no more than a few alphabets
Which to the ear cannot be heard
Yet is all what's seen to the eye

Cameras flashing
Videos replayed
Of Hollywood smiles
And puckered lip selfies
A language of belongingness

An era of toxicity
The only tears welcomed fall from cloudy skies
An era of ingenuity
Friendships held together by strings of likes and followers
A time and place
Where masks are the global language of belongingness

A ripple in time
Rich in empty connections
Where the poor are those without a listening ear
And a comforting smile
Where they drown, unheard and unseen
In a pool of mental conflict.

Powerful*

Perplexed by a loss unforgotten
Overlooked by a mind so tense
Withered to the touch through years of self-defence
Extremities tingled with the sorrows of the crowd
Rivers crossed, just for yourself to accept
Friends helped, most unkept
Under pressure, to everyone unseen
Living days with gloomy smiles, forever obscure.

My Mind

Tiresome thoughts
Bouncing off the walls of my mind
It's hard to believe you're one of a kind

Hollow echoes
Hidden in the crevices of my walls
You stand back up, despite all the falls

Memorable mistakes
Of what once was, is all that I see
I find myself asking, who even was he?

Ease my mind
With your beautiful lies
Show me the way
Without you, I am blind.

Weekend Blues

Weekend blues
Shoes untied
Hair down loose

Bloodshot eyes
Open wide
These lies so hard to recognise

Body surrendered to the beat
Close your eyes
Try to feel complete

Sounds so loud unheard
This reality is absurd
Weekend blues never blurred.

Volume's on too high
Not a care in the world
Melodious tunes slide off luscious lips

The clock's stopped ticking
Oy my mother's yells are so sickening
My father's snores, reassuring

'Cause I've got flavour in my hands
A liver choked off booze
And lungs bruised off what we sniff before we snooze.

Smudge

A pink smudge
In a clear blue sky
A flicker of warmth
Spilling out like hot fudge

Nature's thumbprint
On a good day
Mankind's hint
A pink eye in the sky
Your daily reminder not to die.

Torpidity

Dust and debris danced
In the morning breeze and its cries
Cracked palms shield glassy eyes
Broken nails scratch at bloody fingertips
Toes eaten up by an encroaching blackness

Lungs packed with sand
Respired in high demand
Faces masked against this pandemic's desire
With death tolls only rising higher

Insanity intertwined with lucidity
Tears let loose
And words now have them by a noose
Years lost and lives stolen
Humans left in a state of torpidity.

Murmur

Hearts aflutter
In a sheath built from every stutter
The greying and withered ends of nightmares
Coalesce and caress a beating ruby

Juiced for morning dew
Suffocated in the evening breeze
Hellfire whispers amidst a demanding hurricane

Malice drips in a pool of every beat
A sting and flavour to the midnight worries
Remarks of expectation coughed up
A murmur in the silent cries.

Fluid lies slipped out
Of lips cracked and chewed

Suckling on roses
And dripping honey dew

Glassy eyes from tearful nights
In drunken gazes and hooded sights

A drought of the mind
And a soul that's resigned

All to cover the midnight crazies.

Lips

Small teeth nibbled on my lip
Cherry lips pressed against mine
Breathed rose tea into my being

Soft fingers teased my lower back
My needy hand caressed a faint dimple
Lustrous eyes at a glance seemed so simple

A shy tongue peeked into a bed so warm
Lustful hand grabbed at her spine
To the inside of a heart so crystalline.

Sleep flirtatiously kisses sandy lashes
Dances along hollow sockets
Teasing tired eyes with dreams untold

Fingers intertwined with the prince of fantasies
Through a majesty's palace of drunken lilies
Suckle on these berry lips goodnight

A shadow shivered under the moonlight
A sigh uttered from parted lips
Let go of my hand forever and goodbye.

Hooded eyes
Fingertips clasped a glowing haze
Fog inhaled and sorrows come out in rays

The air whistled its way through
Wasted on cloudy puffs
Lips broke apart

A tight chest for a sunken heart
A bargain worth taking
Bloody dew drips
From cracked drunken lips

Crystals fall from the living room sky
Glittery drizzles shower this mental infidelity
One that can't be mended by any sort of apology.

Inebriated

Thoughts coalesce and combust
Powdering nights in revulsion
Cheeks flushed in anticipation
For more to come
This shan't be discussed, it's a must

Fingers numbed
Lips buzzed
Can't even remember when this begun
Here come the little droplets of rum

Little girl under the stairs
Whatever use are these prayers?
Mommy's inebriated beyond repair
And daddy wasted in despair.

Child

A flicker of red bounced in the sky
String grasped tight, my balloon I'd never let go
Shoes tangled, laces I never know how to tie
Ice cream sliding down my arm
Father's pinkie in my hand
Tiny toes immersed in sand

Why do the moon and sun never get along
Do the clouds taste like cotton candy
What makes a tree so strong?

The waters bubbled and approached
Threatening to spill over the brim
Daddy, daddy, can we go for a swim?